The Chilterns

Nick Channer

COUNTRYSIDE BOOKS
NEWBURY BERKSHIRE

C000165697

First Published 2006
© Nick Channer, 2006

COUNTRYSIDE BOOKS
3 Catherine Road
Newbury, Berkshire

To view our complete range of books,
please visit us at
www.countrysidebooks.co.uk

ISBN 1 85306 962 0
EAN 978 1 85306 962 8

Cover picture of the Hambleden Valley
supplied by John Bethell

Photographs by the author
Designed by Peter Davies, Nautilus Design
Produced through MRM Associates Ltd, Reading
Printed by Information Press Ltd, Oxford

Contents

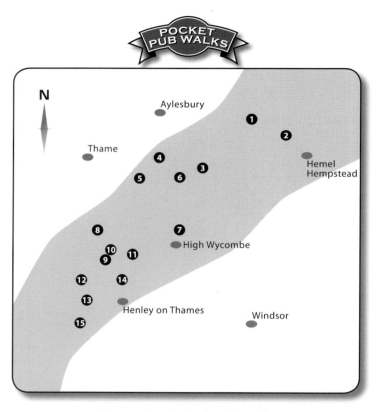

POCKET PUB WALKS

N

Aylesbury

❶

❷

Thame

❹

❸

Hemel Hempstead

❺

❻

❼

❽

High Wycombe

❿

⓫

❾

⓬

⓮

⓭

Henley on Thames

Windsor

⓯

Area map showing location of the walks

Introduction

We have all heard of the Chilterns. But what do we really know about this glorious region of England? When we think of it, we tend to picture rolling hills and dense beechwoods, winding country lanes and hidden villages – and we'd be right. Those of us who love the great outdoors probably define it as an area of the country that cries out to be explored on foot and is the perfect choice for a scenic hiking holiday – and we'd be right to do so too. But there is much more to the Chilterns than walking and magnificent scenery.

Here are a few facts to help broaden your knowledge of this most English of regions. Rising like protective guardians above the Vale of Aylesbury, the Chilterns are in a designated Area of Outstanding Natural Beauty (AONB) covering 308 square miles. The hills are best seen in autumn when the leaves of the beech trees turn from dark green to deep brown. Despite the air of peace and tranquillity and the veneer of green wherever you look, the Chiltern Hills are deceptively close to London – only 35 miles, in fact, from Trafalgar Square. More than 100,000 people live within the Chilterns AONB and there are 50 million visitors a year. One fifth of the area of the Chilterns is covered by woodland – three times the average for England. As well as the familiar beechwoods, the area is renowned for its rare flowers including the Chiltern gentian and the military orchid. From the ground look to the skies and you might well spot red kites. This striking bird of prey was reintroduced in the 1990s and today the Chilterns is home to England's largest population. I could go on forever listing some of the area's lesser-known statistics but hopefully the walks in this pocket guide will give you first-hand knowledge and experience of this unrivalled corner of the country.

These circular routes, which range from 2 to 6¾ miles in length, take you to the heart of the region and uncover some of the less obvious aspects of its history and character. Hopefully, they blend an impressive mix of scenery, family attractions and cultural interest. For example, where else could you be roaming through the Prime Minister's back garden one minute and looking for dead bodies in a quintessential English village the next? Arm yourself with this guide and you'll find out. As well as walks, the other essential ingredient is a good pub and all the routes start and finish at a classic hostelry. Details of food, ales and opening times are featured. If using the pub car park while doing the walk, please consult the landlord first – and you should, of course, be a customer. There is also a note on places of interest in the area so that you can make a day of it if you wish.

Happy walking in the Chilterns!

Nick Channer

Publisher's Note

We hope that you obtain considerable enjoyment from this book; great care has been taken in its preparation. However, changes of landlord and actual closures are sadly not uncommon. Likewise, although at the time of publication all routes followed public rights of way or permitted paths, diversion orders can be made and permissions withdrawn.

We cannot, of course, be held responsible for such diversion orders and any inaccuracies in the text which result from these or any other changes to the routes nor any damage which might result from walkers trespassing on private property. We are anxious though that all details covering the walks and pubs are kept up to date and would therefore welcome information from readers which would be relevant to future editions.

The simple sketch maps that accompany the walks in this book are based on notes made by the author whilst checking out the routes on the ground. However, for the benefit of a proper map, we do recommend that you purchase the relevant Ordnance Survey sheet covering your walk. The Ordnance Survey maps are widely available, especially through booksellers and local newsagents.

1 Aldbury

The Greyhound Inn

This may be a short walk in the Chilterns but it certainly packs in plenty of interest – not least the picturesque village of Aldbury and the tall 1832 Bridgewater Monument rising among the trees on the slopes above. The former is noted for its stocks and pretty pond while the latter, a 108 ft column with 172 steps, commemorates the life and achievements of engineer Francis Egerton, 3rd Duke of Bridgewater (1736–1803), one of the pioneers of Britain's canal system. Egerton worked with designer James Brindley on the 42 mile Bridgewater Canal linking Worsley, Manchester and Runcorn. Known as 'the father of British inland navigation', Egerton was also responsible for the Manchester–Liverpool Canal, completed in 1772. His family owned the Ashridge Estate (see Walk 2) from 1604 until the early 1920s.

The Chilterns

Distance – 2 miles.

OS Explorer 181 Chiltern Hills North. GR 965125.

Field paths and woodland rides outside the village of Aldbury.

Starting point Car park in front of the Greyhound in Aldbury village centre; or the main signposted car park along Stocks Road.

How to get there Take the B4506 to the north of Berkhamsted and follow the signs for Aldbury. As you approach the village centre, turn right into Stocks Road.

THE PUB

One of the best-known pubs in this corner of the Chilterns, the **Greyhound Inn** has undergone an extensive restoration programme. The inn's interior, atmosphere and delightful, classically English setting make it a popular watering hole throughout the year. It is also a firm favourite of passing walkers who can often be found enjoying food in the courtyard on sunny summer days. Among the beers are Badger Best and Tanglefoot. Ciabattas, jacket potatoes and ploughman's lunches feature among the lighter pub fare.

Open 11 am until 11 pm on Monday to Saturday and 12 noon until 10.30 pm on Sunday.
☎ *01442 851228*

1 From the front door of the **Greyhound** turn right, then immediately right along the side of the pub to join the waymarked path. Soon you reach the corner of a field by a kissing gate. Keep right here, with the houses of **Aldbury** over to the right. Keep ahead at the

next kissing gate, following an enclosed path between fencing and hedging. More houses and cottages are seen on the right; on the left is an open field. Pass a sign for the **Percy Crow Path** and on reaching the village sports field make for a pavilion over in the right-hand corner. Follow the path round the back of it to a track leading to **Tring railway station**. Don't take the track – instead, follow the road, which is a few paces to your right, for about 100 yards northwards and turn right at the signpost for **Duncombe Terrace** and **Pitstone**.

2 Cross the stile and follow the field boundary ahead for about 70 yards. Go through the kissing gate in the fence and follow the path across the field, heading for a gate between two houses on the far side. Keep ahead on the footpath and when the track ends, pass through another kissing gate to follow a wide grassy path.

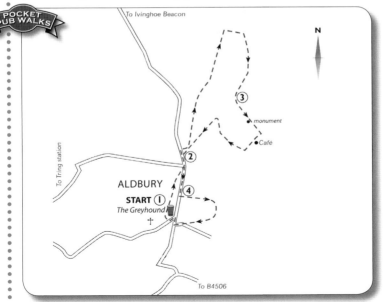

POCKET PUB WALKS

To Ivinghoe Beacon

N

③

● monument

● Café

②

To Tring station

ALDBURY

START ①

The Greyhound

④

To B4506

The Chilterns

Make for a stile in the field corner – field slopes and woodland make up the scene to the right. Keep to the left edge of the next field and follow the path to a kissing gate in the top corner. Turn right and follow a broad path, which runs up into woodland. The path soon curves to the right and climbs steadily. Farther up among the trees a house is visible, the garden partly enclosed by wooden panel fencing.

Aldbury and its village pond.

Veer left at the fork just before it, by a 'no horses' sign, and head further into the woods.

3 Merge with a wide, obvious track and walk towards the **Bridgewater Monument**. Cross the grass to the **Monument Tearoom** and swing right in front of it, following a waymarked bridleway running away from the green and the tearoom. Keep right at the fork and turn sharp right at the first signposted bridleway. Follow the muddy path through trees and undergrowth and soon you'll spot the outline of the monument over to the right. After several minutes or so, on reaching a clearing, look for the roof of a cottage down among the trees on the left. Immediately before you reach a canopy of trees, turn sharp left onto a narrow path running down to the left of the building. Go down the bank and when it meets another path, keep right. Swing left after several paces at the sign for **Aldbury** and drop down very steeply through the woods. Descend carefully towards fields, cross a stile at the bottom and go diagonally left in the pasture. Retrace your steps to the kissing gate, turn right and walk back down to the road. Turn left and head for **Aldbury village centre**.

4 On the outskirts of the village look for a bridleway on the left, signposted to **Northchurch**. Turn left here, pass to the left of a row of cottages and head towards woodland escarpment. As you approach the trees, keep right at a bridleway waymark. Climb quite steeply by various tree roots and after a few paces you come to a junction of bridleways. Take the first right here and follow the sunken path as it curves to the right towards **Aldbury**. At the road turn right, pass the **Aldbury Club** and then turn right into **Stocks Road** for the pub and the car park.

Places of interest nearby

The **Bridgewater Monument** is open to the public between 1 pm and 5 pm at weekends and on bank holidays between April and October.

Located in classic Chiltern country, **Ivinghoe Beacon**, reached by driving north along Stocks Road to Ivinghoe, represents the northern point of the Ridgeway. By visiting the site you can picture this ancient trade route as it used to be when cattle drovers and long-distance pilgrims journeyed along it at the height of summer and in the depths of winter. Some 300 generations have glimpsed the same tracts of chalk downland, the same winding river and the same distant hills.

Close to Ivinghoe Beacon is **Pitstone Windmill**, thought to date back to 1627. The structure is believed to be the oldest surviving windmill in the country. Damaged by a freak storm in 1902, it remained in a derelict state until 1937 when the National Trust acquired it. It has since been restored by volunteers and today is open to the public.
☎ *01494 528051 (Regional Office)*

2 Frithsden

The Alford Arms

If you climbed to the top of the Bridgewater Monument in Walk 1, you'll have looked east across wooded country towards sprawling Ashridge Park. This is one of the route's major highlights, a classic parkland scene dominated by a vast Gothic revival pile noted for its jumble of turrets, towers and battlements. The outward leg of the walk follows well-used paths across commonland and parkland and through extensive beech woodland, while the return is more open, visiting the village of Nettleden en route.

THE PUB The **Alford Arms** is a very popular village pub that attracts drinkers and diners from far and wide. On long summer days it's a real treat to sit outside on the front terrace and enjoy the civilised ritual of afternoon tea. Real ales tend to range from Flowers Original to Marston's Pedigree and the menu is characterised by quality local, free-range and organic produce.

Open Monday to Saturday 11 am to 11 pm; Sunday 12 noon to 10.30 pm.
☎ *01442 864480*

[1] From the front of the pub cross the road and take the path opposite, climbing up through the trees and between bluebell woods. Stay on the broad path, cross a drive and continue beside hedging. Enter more woodland and swing right, keeping right after a few paces to pass alongside trees and private gardens. Soon you come to the fairways of a golf club. Skirt them, keeping to the path as it runs through trees to reach a road.

[2] Cross over, following the **Hertfordshire Way** across more fairways. Pass between trees and farther on you reach a waymarked crossroads. Turn right, following the bridleway down

---

Distance – 6¾ miles.

OS Explorer 181 Chiltern Hills North. GR 016098.

Varied walk in and around delightful and classically English Ashridge Park.

Starting point The Alford Arms at Frithsden.

How to get there *From Hemel Hempstead take the A4146 towards Leighton Buzzard. Pass a pub and a turning for Potten End at Water End and take the next left signposted Frithsden. At the next T-junction turn left and then take a sharp right turning for the village. The Alford Arms is a little way along the lane on the right.*

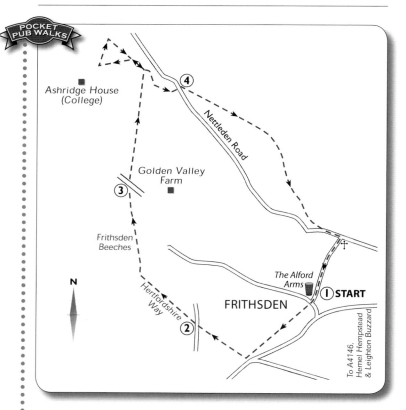

into a dip at **Frithsden Beeches**. Begin ascending the other side and then join a tarmac drive. When it bends right, keep ahead along the field edge and then down through the undergrowth to reach the road.

3 Cross over and take the path signposted to **Little Gaddesden**. Pass the entrance to a house called **Rodinghead** and then follow the path ahead between fences and across rolling parkland. Keep to the left and head down to several beech trees. Cross

the next stile to a track and veer left. After about 120 yards swing left and take the path up the slope to **Ashridge House**. Turn right at the corner of the building and follow the drive to a left-hand bend. Turn right here by a NT bridleway sign and follow the track through the trees and across parkland. Enter woodland and as the track loops dramatically to the left, look for a path running up the bank to an adventure playground. Cross it diagonally to the right corner and turn left at a path T-junction to reach the road.

4 Cross over to a field path and follow it down through a grassy valley. Go over a track and continue through the fields, passing a solitary tree before reaching **Nettleden**. Join the road, pass a waymarked path to **St Margaret's** and turn right a few steps beyond it by Pightle Cottage. Follow the lane and farther up the slope take the woodland path parallel to it on the left. Rejoin the lane and return to the pub.

Places of interest nearby

The 5,000 acre **Ashridge Estate** consists of extensive beech woodland, farmland and open downland now in the care of the National Trust. The house itself was built in 1276 and was restored by James Wyatt in 1808. The **gardens at Ashridge** are open to the public on Saturdays, Sundays and bank holidays between 2 pm and 6 pm from Easter until September.

Chesham Museum, reached on the A416 south of Berkhamsted, contains a small collection of items reflecting the town's unique history of industry and social reform. There are objects from Chesham Cottage Hospital, a 19th century field map and an exhibition of vintage cameras and photographic equipment.
☎ *01494 772096/775798*

3 The Lee

The Cock and Rabbit

he Lee is one of those places, like Mapledurham in south Oxfordshire (Walk 15), that evokes a strong sense of déjà vu. That is because you are bound to have seen the village and its spacious green on the television screen at least once in recent years. It crops up frequently in the ITV detective series *Midsomer Murders* but hopefully you won't find you are knee-deep in corpses when you go there to try this short but very pleasant country walk! The series began in 1997, with the first episode watched by 13.5 million viewers. It's still going strong today. Each one costs something like £1.3 million to make and takes five weeks and about 120 people to film.

THE PUB

The **Cock and Rabbit** has been a pub since 1908. From the outside it has the look and style of a rambling family house – which is what it used to be. Inside it has much to tempt those who love English character inns. Cock and Rabbit cask conditioned bitter and Greene King IPA are the real ales while the appetising bar menu ranges from burger in a bap to spare ribs in a barbecue sauce. There is also a popular Italian restaurant offering pasta, fish and meat dishes.

Open Monday to Saturday 12 noon until 2.30 pm and 6 pm until 11 pm. On Sunday the hours are 12 noon until 3 pm and 7 pm until 10.30 pm.
☎ *01494 837540*

1 From the pub turn left and skirt the green, keeping it on your right. At the next T-junction veer left and enter the churchyard of **St John the Baptist**. The path cuts through the trees to another St John the Baptist, or the **Old Church** as it is known. By the entrance to this historic 13th century building is a stone memorial recalling the life and good works of Captain Bernard Long RN

Distance – 2½ miles.

OS Explorer 181 Chiltern Hills North. GR 898042.

Field paths and woodland to the north and east of The Lee.

Starting point The Cock and Rabbit car park at The Lee.

How to get there *Take the A413 between Wendover and Great Missenden and follow the signs for The Lee. The Cock and Rabbit is on the corner of the large village green.*

The Chilterns

who created the garden adjoining the church and worked in it. He died in 1946. Follow the path round the right-hand bend to a stile. Keep left in the pasture to cross two stiles with a timber-framed building and some barns on the right. In the next field the path forks. Keep right here and head for a galvanised gate and stile on the far side of the pasture. A few paces beyond the stile and gate the path splits. Avoid the path on the immediate left and take the second route – the **Chiltern Link**. Follow the track with hedgerow on the left and open fields on the right towards woodland. Follow the track to the left of the trees and look for a sign 'traps set in this wood'. These days it is unusual to spot such a warning. Continue on the track and, about 120 yards beyond the trees, you'll see a footpath on the right.

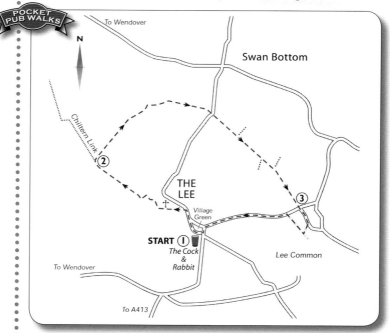

Secluded countryside near The Lee.

2 Take the path and on the far side of the field you cut through a small wood. Continue in the next field with trees and bushes on the left. Look for a white cottage on the left and go to the corner of the pasture. Here you'll find a stile by some holly bushes. Keep right onto the track by the entrance to the cottage, pass a rambling house on the right and merge with its driveway, following it to the road. As you reach it, note a sign that refers to a path by a property (not part of our walk). This invites walkers to 'use a path for your use around the garden', thus avoiding two stiles. Another example of the sort of sign rarely found while out walking in the countryside these days. Cross the road, continue on the woodland path and pass a path and stile on the left. On reaching the next T-junction, avoid the path running off to the right and continue in the same direction. Pass another right of way, this time on the left, running out across fields and when you reach the edge of the wood, cross a stile. Immediately the path forks. Go diagonally across the field and on the far side of the field keep to the right of a hedge and fence.

The Chilterns

3 Cross a stile and at the road beyond it go straight over into **Oxford Street**, following the sign for **Lee Common**. When the road begins to curve left, just before Lee Common Church of England First School, turn right to join a footpath. Veer over to the right in the field and look for a gate leading out to the road. Turn left, pass **The Lee Cricket Club** and walk back to the green at **The Lee**, passing the original, old-style village sign pointing to **Swan Bottom**, **Wendover**, **Great Missenden**, **Lee Common** and **Chesham**.

Places of interest nearby

On the left as you walk towards the **church of St John the Baptist** from the road you'll see the grave of Margaret Rawlings (1906–96), a distinguished thespian and French scholar who was born in Japan and later studied at Lady Margaret Hall, Oxford. She became a professional actress in 1927 and during her working life appeared in a number of films and stage plays. Margaret Rawlings was a founder member of Equity and a passionate conservationist who cared deeply about the countryside. Her husband was Sir Robert Barlow who founded the Metal Box Company in 1943. His grave lies alongside hers. The couple lived locally. Keep an eye out for another gravestone by the path – that of Private R. Dodwell of the Oxford and Bucks Light Infantry who was killed on Boxing Day 1916 aged just 19. The words on his grave seem to symbolise the sheer waste and futility of war. The church is mid-19th century and the churchyard is a conservation area for many insects, birds and mammals. By the door is a brass memorial commemorating Mary Dwight, a devoted servant of the church who was sacristan, verger, sexton, parish clerk and crucifer.

The Bernard Arms

For anyone not familiar with the countryside of the Chilterns region, it may come as something of a surprise to learn that the much-loved Ridgeway long-distance trail cuts through the grounds of Chequers, the Prime Minister's official country retreat. The path crosses the main drive, passing within a few hundred yards of the house. But don't be under any illusion you can wander here at will. There are signs to make sure you follow the correct line of the route and security cameras to capture you on film should you feel the urge to stroll down the drive, pleading confusion as your defence. Chequers dates back to 1565 and was given to the nation in 1921 by Viscount Lee of Fareham. Over the years crucial summits have been held here, Russian presidents have stayed here and many British premiers have wrestled with vital decisions of national importance within its ancient walls. Churchill summed it up best with these words:

The Chilterns

Distance – 5 miles.

OS Explorer 181 Chiltern Hills North. GR 826061.

Paths and tracks through Chequers parkland with glimpses of the great house.

Starting point The Bernard Arms at Great Kimble.

How to get there *Take the A4010 north of Princes Risborough and you'll see the Bernard Arms on the west side of the road when you reach Great Kimble.*

'What distinguished guests it has sheltered, what momentous meetings it has witnessed, what fateful decisions have been taken under this roof.'

THE PUB From the outside the **Bernard Arms** looks like hundreds of pubs throughout Britain. But once you step inside, study the pictures and read the framed newspaper cuttings, you realise this is no ordinary hostelry. The pub's close proximity to Chequers has made it a firm favourite with prime ministers and political leaders over the years. Harold Wilson and his wife Mary called in for a drink on his last Sunday in office in 1976, and John Major brought Boris Yeltsin here during the 1990s, though they were dismayed to find the inn shut! There is even a letter from Tony Blair, dated 1997, thanking the then landlord for inviting the Prime Minister and his family to drop in for a drink though the Blairs have not as yet been seen at the Bernard Arms. Once you've digested all this fascinating information, have a look at the menu, which offers the likes of traditional fish and chips, chef's home-made pie, slow-roasted shoulder of lamb, omelette and trio of local sausages. The beers are Caledonian Deuchars IPA and Adnams Broadside.

Open 12 noon to 3 pm and 6 pm to 10.30 pm on Tuesday, Wednesday and Thursday and 12 noon until 3 pm and 6 pm until 11 pm on Friday and Saturday. On Sunday the hours are 12 noon until 4 pm.
☎ *01844 346172*

1 From the pub turn right, pass **Church Lane** and look for the church and the striking sign for **St Nicholas' church** on the right. It was here, in 1637, that John Hampden (see Walk 6) announced he would not pay Ship Money, therefore taking the country a step closer to the Civil War. Continue along the pavement to a bus stop and lay-by on the right. Cross over opposite the entrance to **Great Kimble House** and just a few yards from it swing left by a cottage with a well. Pass a bewildering proliferation of rights of way and follow the bridleway signposted to the Ridgeway 0.4 miles. This is the route of the **North Bucks Way** and the **Midshires Way**. Take the broad tarmac path uphill, climbing

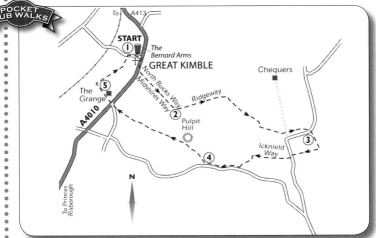

quite steeply through the trees. Pass a footpath on the left, heralded by a wrought iron gate, and continue on the track. Disregard a path on the right, offering very pleasant views, and keep ahead through the trees. Pass a footpath and stile on the right and continue ascending. Soon you join the **Ridgeway**, as indicated by the prominent rights of way post.

2 A few paces beyond it pass through a wrought iron kissing gate and veer diagonally right, still following the **Ridgeway**. Head downhill, using the waymarks to guide you, and pass between trees to begin climbing again. Walk alongside a fence, head up to a kissing gate and continue across the pasture towards trees. You are still on the route of the **Ridgeway**. Keep ahead to a gate and a footpath sign. Look away to the left and you can spy the outline of the monument on distant **Coombe Hill** dedicated to the men of Buckinghamshire who died in the Boer War. Follow the path between fencing and woodland and along this stretch there are fine views of **Chequers** and its surrounding parkland. The path swings right, away from the house, before reaching a **Ridgeway** sign. Turn left here, cut across the field and down towards the main drive and several lodges. Go through two gates, cross the drive and then follow a grassy path between fields.

3 Merge at the road on a bend and cross over to join a lane by some white cottages. Approach some farm outbuildings and look for a clock on the gable end of a barn. Immediately beyond a brick and flint house, turn right to follow a waymarked path running across the fields towards trees. On reaching the road, go straight over, following the **Icknield Way**. Cut through farmland and pass between trees, with final glimpses of **Chequers** on the right. When the woodland becomes more dense, reassuring white arrows guide you through. Cross a track and follow the 'riders' route' down through the trees. Approach a stile leading out to the road. Don't cross it; instead, turn right in front of it and follow the track away from the road. Pass a bridle path on the left after about 50 yards and branch left several steps beyond it to follow a woodland path. At a path T-junction turn left and descend quite steeply through the trees. Keep right on meeting the bridle path and follow it parallel to the road.

4 Keep to the right of a parking area and follow the path through a barrier. Head towards the **Ridgeway**, which is '650 metres' or '0.4 miles' away. Avoid paths running off either side and keep to the broad path, sunken in places. On reaching the **Ridgeway**, where there is a path on the right for **Pulpit Hill Fort**, keep ahead on the bridleway. Merge with a farm access track and at the main road, go straight over and along the drive for **The Grange**. On reaching the house, cross a stile into a paddock and make for its right-hand corner.

5 At this point make sure you pass into the paddock on the right rather than going straight on into the next field. Follow the path across the pasture and then through the grounds of **Old Grange**, following the route of the **North Bucks Way** trail. Cross the fields towards the church at **Great Kimble** and when the path splits, keep left, following the 'circular walk'. Cross the field to a stile that lies to the left of the church. Join a track, go through a galvanised gate and keep to the right of a pond. Keep ahead to a stile leading out to the road and turn right. Walk up to the next T-junction by the church entrance, turn left and return to the pub.

Places of interest nearby

The Roald Dahl Museum and Story Centre at Great Missenden, south-east of Great Kimble, invites visitors to step into the world of one of our most popular authors. Inside you'll find a variety of 'hands on' displays, activities and story-making ideas.
☎ 01494 892192

5 Bledlow

The Lions of Bledlow

A **vast, expansive patchwork** of fields and hedgerows greets the eye as you look towards the Vale of Aylesbury on the outward and return legs of this short, undulating walk. Don't be surprised if occasional cyclists race past you on the Ridgeway and, almost certainly, you'll encounter other ramblers en route. There are several busy junctions of paths

Distance – 2¾ miles.

OS Explorer 181 Chiltern Hills North. GR 776021.

Field paths, tracks and a stretch of the Ridgeway, with views over the clay country of the Vale of Aylesbury.

Starting point The Lions of Bledlow.

How to get there Take the A4010 between High Wycombe and Princes Risborough and follow the signs for Bledlow. On reaching the village, look for the church. The Lions is on the left just beyond it.

along the way. If you are feeling particularly energetic, there is the option to extend the walk to Chinnor Hill where there is a nature reserve.

THE PUB

The Lions of Bledlow is a famous rambling pub overlooking the Vale of Aylesbury. Inside is a charming and atmospheric low-beamed bar, with a log fire to warm you up after a crisp winter walk. In summer you may prefer to sit outside and admire the views and the peaceful village scene. Marston's Pedigree and Wadworth 6X are among the beers found here. The menu offers a good range of bar dishes – everything from traditional ploughman's and home-made pies to vegetarian meals and daily-changing specials.

Open 11.30 am to 3 pm and 6 pm to 11 pm on Monday to Saturday and 12 noon to 3 pm and 7 pm to 10.30 pm on Sunday. Open all day at weekends between May and September.
☎ *01844 343345*

The Chilterns

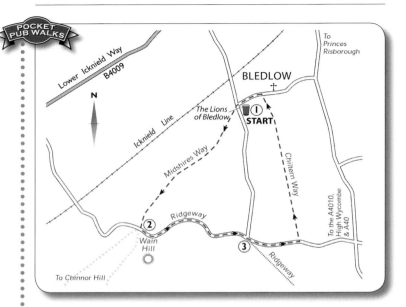

POCKET PUB WALKS

1 From the front of the pub turn left to an immediate junction of paths. On the left is a bridleway leading to the **Ridgeway**. Avoid this and take the wide path or grassy track running across the field. Pass under some power lines and on the far side of the field merge with a track on a bend. Keep ahead, with the wooded bulk of **Wain Hill** and **Bledlow Great Wood** looming above. The track cuts between fences and hedges and begins a gradual climb towards the lower slopes of the hillside. Avoid a footpath running off diagonally right and continue on the track. The views on the right are dominated by the **Vale of Aylesbury**. Soon the track climbs more steeply, heading now for a solitary house up among the trees. Avoid another path on the right, running through trees to a stile and, on reaching the house, you'll see there are several waymarks to guide you.

You can extend the walk to Chinnor Hill from here, if you wish. Use the OS Explorer map to choose your route.

2 *For the main circuit*, turn left to follow the **Ridgeway**, walking along the front of the house and then beside a neat hedge. Beyond the grounds enter woodland and you'll probably spot a sign here 'young trees planted – please keep out'. Follow the broad path along the edge of the woods and along here the outward leg of the walk is glimpsed away to the left. Pass an isolated timber dwelling in the trees and remain on the **Ridgeway**. Avoid a track on the left and when, after a few paces, you break cover from the trees, you'll see a wrought iron gate on the right. The **Ridgeway** leaves the track at this point.

3 Our walk, however, stays on the **Icknield Way** byway. Continue ahead until you reach a path junction. Turn left here over a stile and follow the **Chiltern Way** along the right-hand edge of two

The Chilterns near Bledlow.

fields. Down below the buildings of **Bledlow** can be seen. In the second field corner join an enclosed path between panel fencing to reach the road. To visit the **Holy Trinity church**, turn right for a few paces; to return to the pub turn left and follow the road for a short distance.

Places of interest nearby

The **Ridgeway** is Britain's oldest road and one of our most famous and best-loved long distance trails. Officially opened by the Countryside Commission in 1973 and originally an important trade route, the path runs for a total of 85 miles between Ivinghoe Beacon at the northern end of the Chilterns and Avebury in Wiltshire. The character of the Ridgeway is split by the River Thames. On the Chilterns bank, the scenery is wooded with swathes of rolling hillside – typical of the area. Through Berkshire, Oxfordshire and Wiltshire, the views of the chalk landscape never seem to change and for long stretches there is little or no shelter from the elements. However, exploring this exposed section of the route on foot usually evokes a wonderful sense of space, solitude and distance.

West Wycombe House, south-east of Bledlow and reached on the A40, is one of the locations in the latest film version of Oscar Wilde's *The Importance of Being Earnest*, starring Judi Dench. It dates back to the 18th century and was built for Sir Francis Dashwood, founder of the Dilettanti Society and the notorious Hellfire Club. The house and gardens are now owned by the National Trust and can be viewed in the summer. The nearby caves, extended to a depth of 1,320 ft in the 1750s by Sir Francis to provide work for local people, are privately owned and National Trust members are required to pay an admission fee.
☎ *01494 513569*

6 **Great Hampden**

The Hampden Arms

Two **famous men** are closely associated with this lovely woodland walk – one a gentleman landowner and significant figure in the English Civil War, the other a famous First World War poet. John Hampden, a noted Parliamentarian and MP for Buckinghamshire, lived at Hampden House which features in the closing stages of the walk. Hampden was vehemently opposed to the Ship Money, a tax levied by Charles I for outfitting the navy, and was prosecuted before the Court of Exchequer in 1637. He played a key role in the Parliamentary opposition to Charles and during the Civil War helped to raise a regiment of infantry for the Roundheads. He was killed in battle at Chalgrove Field near Thame in 1643. Rupert Brooke and his friends, including the actress Cathleen Nesbitt, stayed at an inn on the route of this walk called the Pink and Lily. It was their base and from here they would wander off to explore the surrounding countryside on foot, sometimes dining al fresco at the side of the path. Brooke was even inspired to include the pub in a rhyming couplet:

> 'Never came there to the Pink
> Two such men as we I think;
> Never came there to the Lily
> Two men quite so richly silly.'

But where does the name originate? According to some sources, Mr Pink and Miss Lily were butler and maid at Hampden House and they eventually came to live in this building before it was a pub.

THE PUB From the outside, the **Hampden Arms** looks more like a private house than a pub. However, its mock Tudor style and semi-wooded setting are familiar to walkers and motorists alike. Inside the atmosphere is cosy and inviting. Beers include Hook Norton, Adnams and Boddingtons and the lunchtime

---

Distance – 5 miles.

OS Explorer 181 Chiltern Hills North. GR 845015.

Woodland paths and tracks through the wooded Hampden Estate.

Starting point – The Hampden Arms car park.

How to get there Follow any of the unclassified roads across country between Princes Risborough and Great Missenden and take the signposted turning for Great Hampden. The pub is in the village centre.

Great Hampden

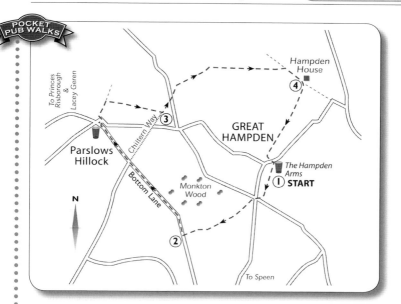

snack menu might feature steak sandwich, shepherd's pie, omelette, baked cod and yellow fin sole. The restaurant offers more substantial fare if that is your preference.

Open 12 noon to 3 pm and 6 pm to 11 pm between Monday and Saturday. Sunday hours are 12 noon until 3 pm and 7 pm until 10.30 pm.
☎ *01494 488255*

1 From the pub turn left, then left again into Memorial Road. Veer right after a few steps, by a bus stop, and follow the waymarked path, keeping along the right-hand boundary of the cricket ground. Make for an opening in the trees and cross a stile into woodland. Follow the path through the trees, keeping a field on the right. Descend through the woods to reach the road and

turn right to a junction. Cross over to the road for **Speen** and take the bridleway on the corner. Head uphill through the trees and continue ahead on the higher ground, following the path through extensive mixed woodland. Pass over a ride and keep ahead. Farther on, you glimpse fields ahead beyond the trees. This stretch of the walk evokes a curious sense of solitude and isolation. Emerge from the woods and continue on a clear path between wooden fencing and fields.

2 After about 150 yards you reach a junction. Turn right here and follow Lily Bottom Lane as it runs between trees and hedges. Pass a footpath on the left and continue on the track. In a while look for a brick and flint house on the right followed by **The Barn**. Soon the **Chiltern Way** crosses your path; keep ahead on the lane to **Parslows Hillock**. At the junction, with **Wardrobes Lane** opposite, turn left to visit the **Pink and Lily pub**; to continue the walk turn right and follow the road to a right bend. At this point veer left, following the bridleway signs, and bend right by the entrance to **Hampton Lodge**. Head north through the woods and after a minute or two you reach a footpath on the right. Take the path and pass through glorious sprawling woodland. Cross over a ride where there is a waymark and at the next track, just before some fir trees, swing half right at the waymark to pass alongside holly trees.

3 Soon you come to a stile by a cottage called **Wood View**. Cross over to the road and turn left, following the 'circular walk' sign. Keep left at the junction for several paces and then turn right onto the **Chiltern Way**. Cross a stile and follow the path along the top of a bank. Continue through the woods and when you reach a waymarked fork, keep right. Stay on the **Chiltern Way**, passing occasional waymarks and shortly you'll see fields ahead in the distance. On reaching the edge of farmland, head diagonally right towards a sizeable clump of trees beyond which is **Hampden House** and its church. The façade of the house is mid-18th century Gothic with the original house behind it

dating back to the 14th century. Pass through the trees and continue on the obvious path to the far side of the field. Cross a track, go through a gate and continue towards the house. Avoid a stile on the left, pass through the next gate and alongside the rather striking Gothic stable block.

Hampden House is passed on the walk.

4 Beyond it is the parish church of **St Mary Magdalen**, which dates from about the same period as the house. Turn right into the churchyard and look for the unusual Oliver family plot. Go through a kissing gate and ahead across several fields, passing through a series of gates. Cross a farm access road and then continue ahead on an unfenced path running across open fields. The houses of **Great Hampden** are visible now. Pass alongside light woodland and keep ahead to a drive leading to some houses. Go straight on and after a few moments the **Hampden Arms** is seen in the near distance. Follow the grassy path directly to it.

Places of interest nearby

Lacey Green Windmill, south-west of Parslows Hillock, has machinery dating from about 1650. The windmill has been restored to working order by the Chiltern Society and is open from the beginning of May until the end of September on Sundays and Bank Holidays from 2.30 pm until 5.30 pm.

7 Downley

The Le De Spencers Arms

This delightful walk evokes the memory of a distinguished Victorian Prime Minister, Benjamin Disraeli, who lived for many years at Hughenden Manor to the north of High Wycombe. He loved this corner of the Chilterns and in particular the peaceful wooded countryside to the north-west of the house, explored by this walk. Much of the route is under cover of trees, which provide welcome shade on a hot day and respite when the weather turns unexpectedly wet.

THE PUB — As a village pub, the **Le De Spencers Arms** has the rare distinction of being hidden away from the hub of the community, halfway along a track lined by private houses. Many walkers stumble upon it by accident and are only too pleased to break their journey here, regarding it as a

Distance – 2 miles.

OS Explorer 172 Chiltern Hills East. GR 848957.

Woodland paths and tracks close to the grounds of Hughenden Manor.

Starting point The Le de Spencers Arms by the common at Downley.

How to get there *From the A40 between High Wycombe and West Wycombe, turn off northwards at the sign for Downley. Drive towards the village but avoid turning right for its centre. Instead, keep ahead alongside The Common and then follow the road round to the right. Where it meets a track by a row of houses, turn left and drive along to the pub, which is on the right.*

conveniently sited watering hole in the midst of the Chiltern countryside. The building is thought to date back over 400 years and at one time it traded as a bakery. There is an extensive menu, offering the likes of pizza, baguettes, scampi and chips, pies and steaks, and a good range of real ales – Fuller's Chiswick, London Pride and ESB among them.

Open Monday to Thursday from 12.30 pm to 3.30 pm and 6 pm to 11 pm; Friday and Saturday from 12 noon until 11 pm; Sunday 12 noon until 10.30 pm.
☎ *01494 535317*

1 From the pub turn right and follow the track as it runs alongside various properties. When they end, pass between wooden posts and follow the waymarks into woodland. Once inside, veer over

The Chilterns

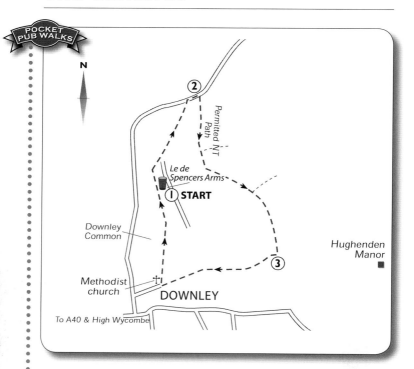

POCKET PUB WALKS

N

② ↑

Permitted NT Path

Le de Spencers Arms

① START

Downley Common

Hughenden Manor

③

Methodist church ✝

DOWNLEY

To A40 & High Wycombe

to the right, keeping a bungalow and garden on the right through the trees. Go straight on at a waymark, avoiding a left-hand path, and keep to the right-hand edge of the wood. Pass a gate on the right and continue through the trees. Chiltern downland and fields are visible between the branches along this stretch of the walk. Hug the woodland edge to a minor road and turn right. After about 100 yards look for a kissing gate on the right.

② Take the path, signposted '**Hughenden Manor**', and follow it down the middle of the field. Soon it curves to the left and reaches double gates. Continue ahead through the woods, passing a path to **Naphill** on the left. Keep on the wide path as it cuts through the heart of the woodland, avoid a path on the left and look for fields ahead through the trees. As you reach the edge of the pasture, pass a path on the right for **Downley Common** and go forward through a galvanised gate. Cross the field to the next gate and turn right for **Downley**.

3 Follow the bridle track through farmland and soon you enter woods again. Keep on the main path and begin a gradual gentle ascent. Farther on you come to a National Trust sign for the Hughenden Estate (**Manor Farm**). Continue ahead, slightly left. As you emerge from the trees in a short while, you'll see the **Methodist church**, dated 1824. Look for the centenary memorial stone laid by an Arthur Fairfax of Banbury. Other stones can be seen in the wall. In fact, there are so many to read,

National Trust land near Downley.

The Chilterns

it could delay the end of your walk! Turn right here, go up the short stony slope and pass a **Downley Millennium yew tree**, planted in 2000. Cross the common, veering over to the right to join a track by a line of houses. Keep them on the right and when the road comes in from the left, walk ahead to the pub.

Places of interest nearby

Hughenden Manor is a short distance from the main walk. Using the OS Explorer map, it is easy to extend the route in order to visit Disraeli's former home and its lovely parkland, now the property of the National Trust. Queen Victoria's favourite Prime Minister was born in 1804 and entered parliament, representing Maidstone, in 1837. Looking at the manor and its glorious setting, it's not difficult to see why he chose this as his country seat in 1848. By the time he and his wife moved here, Disraeli was an established novelist as well as a prominent figure in British politics. He became Chancellor of the Exchequer in Lord Derby's three successive ministries and was Prime Minister in the 1860s and 70s. After his wife died in 1872, Disraeli remained at Hughenden until his death in 1881. Undoubtedly he will always be credited with using his patience and skilful persuasion to coax Queen Victoria back into public life after the death of Prince Albert. Though he died twenty years before her, at the time of his passing he was one of her closest confidants. The house is Georgian, though it was given a Gothic flavour in 1862. Inside are many of Disraeli's books and pictures, together with a number of letters from Queen Victoria who spent some time in his study after his funeral. Particularly impressive are the gardens at Hughenden, designed by Disraeli's wife Mary Anne.
☎ 01494 755565 (infoline)

8 Christmas Common

The Fox & Hounds

According to various sources, the remote hamlet of Christmas Common takes its name from a notable day in the history of the Civil War. By Christmas 1643 the Parliamentarians held nearby Watlington, while the Royalists defended the ridge on which Christmas Common is situated. In view of the nature and significance of the occasion, a temporary truce was apparently called and both armies met on this spot during the festivities. Hence the unusual and rather charming name. Starting at Christmas Common, the walk soon offers magnificent views down towards Watlington, Didcot and across a wide sweep of Oxfordshire countryside. The vistas from Watlington Park, near the end, are equally memorable.

The Chilterns

Distance – 2½ miles.

OS Explorer 171 Chiltern Hills West. GR 714932.

Classic beechwoods in the vicinity of Watlington Park.

Starting point The Fox & Hounds at Christmas Common.

How to get there Follow the A4130 between Henley and Wallingford and branch northwards onto the B481 at Nettlebed. Turn right onto the B480 and then immediately left for Christmas Common. The pub will be found on the left after about 2 miles.

THE PUB

The **Fox & Hounds** has been extensively refurbished and this 500-year-old pub offers customers a smart interior and a spacious restaurant. An open-plan kitchen, a cosy fire on cold days and four intimate bar areas add to the appeal. On the wide-ranging and very appetising menu you'll find the likes of Welsh rarebit, Scottish smoked salmon sandwich with cream cheese and cucumber, local venison and cep casserole and braised lamb shank. Beers include Brakspear Bitter and several guest ales.

Open 11.30 am to 3 pm and 6 pm to 11 pm on Monday to Friday; all day Saturday and Sunday though the pub is closed on Sunday afternoons between November and March.
☎ *01491 612599*

1 From the **Fox & Hounds** turn left and follow the road. Pass a turning to **North End** and continue towards **Stokenchurch** and **Chinnor**. Avoid a footpath on the right and walk between white

gates and a 'weak bridge' sign. A few paces beyond it swing left at the sign for **Watlington**. Pass the speed de-restriction sign and keep to the straight road running between hedgerows. After about 100 yards veer left at the footpath sign and go through a gate. On the horizon are the familiar shapes of the cooling towers at **Didcot Power Station**, their clouds of steam drifting lazily over the Oxfordshire countryside.

2 Swing right for a few paces towards a gate. Don't go through it; instead, follow the path along the field boundary, keeping it on your right. Pass through trees and then along the edge of fields. Look out for deer skipping among the trees and across the open pasture. Continue for some time along the perimeter of the woodland and look for white arrows, waymarks and National Trust signs. Join a track at **Lower Dean**, pass a barn conversion and the old farmhouse and continue along the access

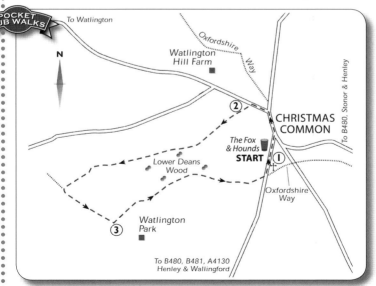

The Chilterns

track to another house. Beyond it is a map of the **Watlington Park Estate**, showing rights of way and other features. Turn left at the T-junction and after a few paces the track bends right into the trees. At this point go straight on uphill to a gate at the edge of the wood. Go straight ahead up the steep grassy track towards trees. At the top there is a glorious view across a wide sweep of Oxfordshire.

3 Enter the woodland and swing left after several steps. On your right you can see the façade of **Watlington Park** framed by trees. Follow the path ahead through the woods – here and there are glimpses of rolling Chiltern country. Veer right at one point and continue between trees to reach a drive. Turn left for the road and left again. Pass the little **church of the Nativity**, dating back to 1889 on the right and return to the pub.

Places of interest nearby

Watlington is one of Oxfordshire's prettiest towns and a good base for exploring the Chilterns. Its history dates back to the Civil War and beyond, with Royalist and Parliamentarian armies fighting each other in the surrounding countryside. One of Watlington's most notable landmarks is the gabled **Town Hall**, built in 1664. It is known to be one of the oldest in the country and was originally constructed as a market hall, built with funds donated by a Mr Thomas Stonor. The upper room was converted into a grammar school for boys until 1872. The town has a strong 18th century look about it, yet many of its streets were already complete by the 14th century. Chalk used as building material in the town's early development came from pits at the foot of the Chilterns. Local people were given special rights, including quarrying their own chalk for constructing houses.

9 Upper Maidensgrove

The Five Horseshoes

A **Site of Special Scientific Interest**, the Warburg Reserve near Maidensgrove is a haven of ancient woodland and flower-rich grassland. Named after an Oxford botanist, the reserve straddles a dry, winding valley and the pooling of cold air along the valley floor means that from time to time very severe frosts leave their mark on this delightful corner of the countryside. In summer the air is filled with the song of numerous birds and below the branches of the trees the ground is a richly textured carpet of wild flowers. Orchids and bluebells and more than 900 species of fungi thrive here. Look for deer browsing in the peaceful glades. In autumn the colours at the Warburg Reserve are glorious, particularly on a bright day in October when the leaves are beginning to turn and the sun bathes the surroundings in a glorious mellow light.

THE PUB Dating back to the 17th century, the **Five Horseshoes** occupies one of the prettiest settings in the Chilterns. From its two beer gardens there are lovely views across open country towards the Warburg Reserve, the focal point of this delightful walk. Inside the pub, there is plenty to occupy you and help you relax after the physical demands of a Chiltern ramble. There are traditional pub games, a welcoming atmosphere, two snug bar areas and an assortment of home-cooked traditional dishes – including a platter of rustic breads, soup, beer-battered fish and chips, shepherd's pie, bangers and mash and casserole of 'free range' chicken. Brakspear Bitter and Special are among the real ales.

Distance – 4½ miles.

OS Explorer 171 Chiltern Hills West. GR 711891.

A walk to a secluded nature reserve criss-crossed by various paths and tracks. But be warned – after rain the wet leaves can conceal deep ruts and puddles.

Starting point The Five Horseshoes at Upper Maidensgrove.

How to get there From the A4130 between Henley and Wallingford, join the B480 at Lower Assendon and make for Stonor. Turn left for Maidensgrove and Russell's Water and the pub will be found on the left after several miles. The car park is across the road, opposite the inn.

Open 12 noon to 3.30 pm and 6 pm to 11 pm from Monday to Friday; Saturday hours are 12 noon until 11 pm and Sunday 12 noon until 6 pm.
☎ *01491 641282*

1 From the pub car park turn left and pass a sign for **Maidensgrove and Russell's Water Commons**. Note that 'motorcycles and motor vehicles are not allowed more than 15 feet from the public highway and the flying of powered model aircraft is expressly forbidden'. Follow the grassy track parallel to the road and beside the common, pass a farm on the right and continue along the lane. Beyond the 30 mile per hour speed restriction sign, where the road bends left, swing right to join a signposted public right of way. Avoid a path running off to the south-west

The Chilterns

and continue on the main path. Descend to an information board about **Warburg** – a map here shows the paths and nature trails within the boundaries of the reserve. Cross the signposted **Wildlife Walk** and keep ahead down the broad path. Pass another trail on the left and after about 70 yards, you reach a junction with a track.

2 Turn left and pass between trees en route to the **Warburg visitor centre** and picnic area. Walk between them and along the track to a brick and timber-framed cottage on the right. This is **Pages Farm**. Turn right immediately beyond it, following the track as

it begins a gentle ascent. Keep left farther up at a fork – there is also a path running off sharp right here – and begin climbing more steeply. Pass another information board for **Warburg** as you reach the edge of the reserve. At this stage of the walk the track passes beneath a thick canopy of beech trees before reaching a track running off half right. Avoid it and continue beside wooden panel fencing. On reaching the

Warburg Reserve near Maidensgrove.

entrance to **Soundess House** on the left, turn right and skirt the woodland on a wide track. **Soundess Farm** can be seen on the left. When the track bends sharp right, go straight on along a field path, following the **Chiltern Way**.

3 Some way along the boundary you'll see two stiles and a waymark half hidden in the trees on the right. Cross them and keep ahead under the branches of trees and alongside fencing. Cross a stile and at this point try and pick out the buildings of **Upper Maidensgrove** up on the hillside. Go diagonally across the field and drop down to a stile in the bottom boundary. At the junction immediately beyond the stile go straight over and follow the sometimes muddy path between trees and hedges. Keep ahead until you reach a junction of paths.

4 On the left is the **Chiltern Way**; on the right is **Shakespeare's Way**, a new long-distance path exploring the countryside between Stratford-upon-Avon and the Globe Theatre on London's South Bank. Take the latter path and climb steeply up the hillside. The ascent is thankfully short and soon the path curves right. After a few paces you'll see a stile on the left. Cross it and then go up a steep bank for a few paces to two more stiles. Walk ahead towards a house, keeping to the left of it on the enclosed path. Cross a stile leading out to the road, turn right and return to the pub.

Places of interest nearby

The nearby town of **Wallingford** has plenty to capture your attention. Once an important river crossing, this is where William the Conqueror built a large castle to protect it. During the Civil War, the 11th century fortification was the last Royalist stronghold in Oxfordshire to surrender, following a brave Parliamentary siege lasting over 60 days. Cromwell later ordered the castle to be demolished. Look out, too, for the **Town Hall**, one of Wallingford's finest buildings, and the town's six churches – there used to be 16! Before leaving, visit **Wallingford Museum**, which includes a time-warp walk through the Saxon and medieval periods. Also on display are a Victorian shop, a pub and a model of Wallingford station.

The Crown

The **Oxfordshire Way**, which was officially opened in 1976, is still one of the best ways to explore the southern half of the Chilterns. Linking the region with the Cotswolds, it was originally conceived by the CPRE (Council for the Protection of Rural England) with help from the Oxfordshire branch of the Ramblers' Association and the Oxford Fieldpaths Society. This walk follows part of the trail against an ever-changing backdrop of softly rolling hillsides and extensive beechwoods. With just one short stretch of road at the start and finish, it's the perfect 'getaway from it all' walk. The last time I trod this path my only companions were red kites circling overhead and a solitary rambler who asked me for directions.

Distance – 4 miles.

OS Explorer 171 Chiltern Hills West. GR 725901.

Isolated paths and tracks through spectacular Chilterns country.

Starting point The Crown at Pishill.

How to get there From the A4130 between Henley and Wallingford, turn northwards onto the B480 at Lower Assendon. Follow the road through Stonor and continue to Pishill. The Crown will be found on the right in the village street.

THE PUB

According to some sources, the **Crown** is haunted by the ghost of a priest who hid in the pub's priest hole and later committed suicide. During the 'flower power' era of the 1960s, however, this was the haunt of showbusiness celebrities and pop stars rather than spirits fleeing religious persecution. Among those visiting the Crown were Dusty Springfield, George Harrison and Ringo Starr who performed in the trendy nightclub housed in the adjoining barn. Brakspear's is the favourite beer here and the menu offers something for everyone.

Open 11.30 am until 2.30 pm and 6 pm until 11 pm on Monday to Saturday. Sunday hours are 12 noon until 3 pm and 7 pm until 10.30 pm.
☎ *01491 638364*

1 On leaving the pub turn left and follow the road for several hundred yards, taking care as there is no pavement along this stretch. However, the road is relatively quiet most of the time. Turn right at the sign for the **Oxfordshire Way** to have a look at

The Chilterns

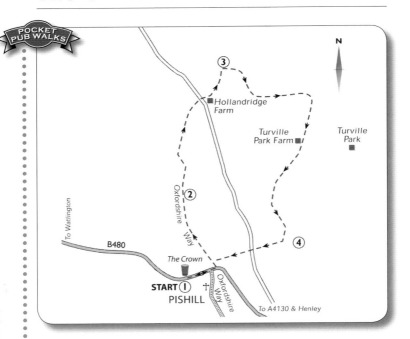

Map showing the walk route, featuring: N compass, Hollandridge Farm, Turville Park Farm, Turville Park, Oxfordshire Way, B480, To Watlington, The Crown, START (1) PISHILL, Oxfordshire Way, To A4130 & Henley, and numbered points (2), (3), (4).

Pishill church. Return to the B480 and turn right. As the road bends right, turn left by a gate for **Pishill Farm** to join a track carrying the route of the **Oxfordshire Way**. After a few paces, as the track veers left, keep ahead on the main route. Follow the trail through a shallow, dry valley and along this stretch you may catch sight of an occasional red kite circling overhead. Trees cloak the upper slopes of the valley. Head towards a curtain of woodland and when you reach a dilapidated stile by the trees, look for hand-painted white arrows and **Oxfordshire Way** symbols to guide you.

2 Keep right at the fork, which is reached after a few paces, and begin a moderate but quite lengthy climb up the hillside through the trees. More arrows can be seen on the tree trunks. At length

the outline of **Hollandridge Farm** can be seen in the distance. Avoid a path running off to the left just before the edge of the woods and go straight on to a stile leading into a field. Keep right and on reaching a stile in the corner, continue ahead along the right-hand edge of the field. On reaching the hedge corner, strike out on the clear path across the pasture and drop down the slope towards woodland. Pass into the trees, following a section of the **Chiltern Way** and the **Oxfordshire Way**. Keep ahead until you reach a junction of paths where you turn right.

3 Follow the broad, clear path through the woods, passing various waymarks and white arrows. Farther on the trees thin and here there are glimpses of rolling Chiltern pastures. Pass alongside paddocks, following the path as it curves gradually to the right. The buildings of **Turville Park Farm** can be seen ahead now. On the left are extensive woods and along this stretch you can read how the trees here were planted and established to provide timber for the furniture industry, then based in High Wycombe. Pass an avenue of trees leading to **Turville Park** and continue ahead on a path between fields and paddocks. Cross a stile and keep ahead; in time the path widens to a track and then crosses a boundary into the adjoining field. Continue in a southerly direction and when white arrows and a hay barn are seen, turn right.

The view from Pishill churchyard.

The Chilterns

4 Follow the path, part of the **Stonor Estate**, as it runs up the slope towards trees on the skyline. On reaching a track, go straight over and on along a path towards **Pishill**. Follow the field boundary and as it starts to curve to the right, keep left, passing through a wrought iron gate. The path passes alongside **Pishill Farmhouse** to reach a stile. Turn left for the road, swing right and return to the pub.

Places of interest nearby

Just a couple of minutes or so from the route of the walk lies **Pishill church**. Unusually, this is one of very few churches in the country without a dedication. Dating back to before the Reformation, the church contains an aisle to the Stonor family who were staunch Catholics. The beautiful window in the chancel was unveiled in 1969 and is the work of John Piper. It shows St Paul's emblems, the Sword and the Gospel, with the Gospel held open by two hands in front of the Sword.

Near to Pishill is **Stonor Park**, which is open to the public at certain times of the year. There has been a house here since the Norman Conquest – the present one dates from the end of the 12th century and has been enlarged and restored a great many times over the years. The Chapel of the Holy Trinity is 14th century and it was here, in 1580, that Lady Stonor gave refuge to the Jesuit priest and martyr Edmund Campion, who was later arrested and executed at Tyburn. The house contains sculptures, tapestries, drawings, paintings and many items of fine furniture. Stonor also includes a medieval Catholic chapel, which was in constant use during the Catholic repression. There are several footpaths running through Stonor Park so walkers are at liberty to stroll in the grounds all through the year.
☎ *01491 638587*

11 Skirmett

The Frog

As you stroll through the picturesque village of Turville on this glorious Chilterns walk, you may get that feeling that you have been here before. Maybe you have. Or perhaps you recognise it from its countless appearances in films and television productions over the years – most notably *The Vicar of Dibley*, the BBC comedy series, and the award-winning ITV drama *Goodnight Mister Tom* starring the late John Thaw. Turville even featured in a black and white propaganda film of the early

The Chilterns

Distance 3 miles.

OS Explorer 171 Chiltern Hills West. GR 775903.

Undulating woodland, field paths and glorious views in the countryside surrounding the village of Turville.

Starting point The Frog pub at Skirmett.

How to get there Take the A4155 between Henley and Marlow and head north at Mill End, passing through Hambleden. On reaching Skirmett, you'll find the Frog on the left

1940s, *Went the Day Well*, based on a short story by Graham Greene. Another movie, *Chitty Chitty Bang Bang*, was filmed in the area, much of it at Cobstone Mill on the hill overlooking Turville. Just before reaching the village, you'll see a footpath sign advising walkers that the land here is owned by Turville Court Estate and managed organically with wildlife conservation and biodiversity in mind. As you approach Fingest, the landscape crossed in the early stages of the walk – a mixture of rolling hills and woodland – can be seen nearby.

THE PUB From the garden of the **Frog**, a lovely family-owned pub, there are pretty views over the Chilterns. Inside the scene is equally impressive. The bar has a welcoming fire in winter and the popular restaurant offers a well-designed menu with dishes changing monthly. There are also daily specials on the blackboard. Beers include Adnams Best, Rebellion IPA and a guest ale. When tackling this glorious walk to Turville and back in the depths of winter, you might feel in need of a warming bowl of home-made soup. Alternatively, try an appetising baguette or baked marrow and ratatouille topped with goat's cheese.

Skirmett Walk 11

Open 11.30 am to 3 pm and 6.30 pm to 11 pm from Monday to Saturday. On Sundays in summer the pub is open from 12 noon until 10.30 pm; between October and May the Frog is open between 12 noon and 4 pm.
☎ *01491 638996*

1 From the pub car park turn left, passing a cottage with the appropriate name of '**Ramblers**'. Continue through the village and take the next footpath on the left, where there is a 'private drive' sign. Cut through an avenue of trees, avoid the stile and footpath on the right-hand side by a tennis court and keep along the drive. Look away to the right for a first glimpse of **Cobstone Mill** up on the hillside. At the end of the drive keep

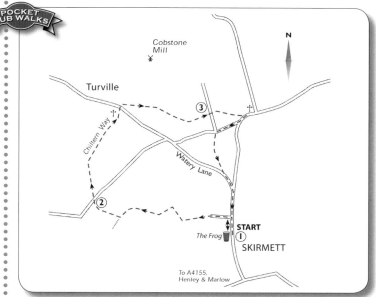

The Chilterns

The picturesque village of Turville.

ahead over a stile. Dilapidated barns can be seen on the right here. Climb steeply uphill through the fields towards woodland, following the path as it bends sharp right further on by the trees. Swing left shortly and keep climbing through glorious Chiltern beechwoods. When the path forks, veer right as requested by the waymarks and follow the broad obvious path through the woodland. At the next T-junction and waymark, turn right and descend between the trees. Emerging from them, continue down on a grassy path to more woodland and join a track serving a gas installation.

2 At the road cross over to a stile and aim diagonally right, following the field path up to the top boundary. When you reach a fence, keep right following the **Chiltern Way**, passing a gate on the left. Continue down to the field corner, go through a gate and follow the enclosed path between trees to the edge of **Turville**.

Keep ahead into the village and on reaching the green at its centre, cross the road and pass to the right of the **Old School House**. Follow the **Chiltern Way** to a stile and here the path forks. Swing right, taking the lower path along the grassy flanks of the hillside. Away up to the left is **Cobstone Mill**. Cross a stile and cut between trees and fencing.

3 Follow the path to a road, cross over and continue through trees. Avoid a path running off to the left and keep ahead down to **Fingest church**. Turn right at the road and soon you reach a junction. Keep right, signposted **Turville**, and pass a row of houses on the left. Immediately beyond, opposite a turning for **Ibstone** and **Stokenchurch**, turn left to join a path running across the field. Continue across several more pastures until you see a cottage and the road ahead. Go through a gate and ahead along the road, back into **Skirmett**.

Places of interest nearby

The town of **Marlow** is packed with things to see and do. West Street was once the home of the poet Shelley, whose wife Mary wrote her classic story *Frankenstein* here. It was published in 1818. Another celebrated literary figure, T. S. Eliot, lived at Marlow between 1917 and 1920. The town's famous suspension bridge was completed in 1832, having been designed by William Tierney Clark who was inspired by similar constructions he had seen at Hammersmith and in Budapest. This bridge is the only surviving example of his work. Across the river lies the **Compleat Angler**, a famous hotel boasting Clint Eastwood, Naomi Campbell and Omar Sharif among its celebrity guests over the years. In July, Marlow is home to the ancient ceremony of Swan Upping and in mid-June the town holds the Marlow Regatta and Festival in Higginson Park.

12 **Highmoor**

The Dog and Duck

Almost **immediately after leaving the pub** you enter a peaceful world of sprawling woodland and rolling Chiltern farmland. Midway round is the village of Stoke Row, noted for a picturesque pub, the Crooked Billet. It was here that Reading-born actress Kate Winslet held her first wedding reception. Dick Turpin, surely more infamous than famous, reputedly hid here during his reign as a much-feared highwayman. Nearby is a rather unusual but very moving tribute to a man who clearly loved this glorious part of the world.

THE PUB

The **Dog and Duck** is how pubs used to be – unspoiled and unpretentious. Among the features inside are panelled walls, stained glass in the doors, a beamed ceiling and a cosy fire on cold days. There are also photographs of the pub in the 1930s, including a hunting scene and a charabanc trip. You will find several bars and a dining area where you can enjoy dishes such as pie, mash and chips, quiche, Cornish pasty or lamb shank. For something lighter there is a choice of sandwiches. In the summer the large garden soon fills up with customers who enjoy the timeless appeal of this delightful old Chiltern inn.

In winter the pub is open from 11.30 am until 10 pm on Monday, Tuesday and Wednesday; 11.30 am until 11 pm on Thursday, Friday and Saturday; 12 noon until 3 pm on Sunday. Summer hours are 11 am until 11 pm every day, including Sunday. There is no hot food on Mondays throughout the year.
☎ *01491 641261*

Distance – 4 miles, but you may like to cut it short by about ½ mile. At present the longer route includes a high stile, which some walkers and quite a few dogs might find difficult to negotiate.

OS Explorer 171 Chiltern Hills West. GR 701847.

Fine mix of classic Chiltern countryside – extensive woodland and rolling farmland.

Starting point The Dog and Duck at Highmoor.

How to get there *Take the B481 between Reading and the A4130. The pub is on the east side of the road just to the south of Nettlebed.*

The Chilterns

1 From the **Dog and Duck** turn right along the B481 for a few paces, following the broad grassy verge. Turn left to join a footpath by the sign for **Appletree Cottage**. Pass to the right of the cottage and follow the path alongside wooden panel fencing. Negotiate a stile, then cross a small field to a stile and enter woodland. Cut between trees and holly bushes and when you reach a major intersection, look for the corner of wooden panel fencing a few yards away. Cross over the junction and keep the fencing on your left, passing through a gate. Laurel bushes can be seen along this stretch. Keep the buildings and boundary fence of **Highmoor Farm** on the left. Make for a stile and go forward for 50 yards to the next stile. Walk down the field edge, keeping trees on the right, and aim for a gateway and stile in the field corner. Go slightly left down the steep field slope to another stile and gateway. Pass into the next pasture and go diagonally up

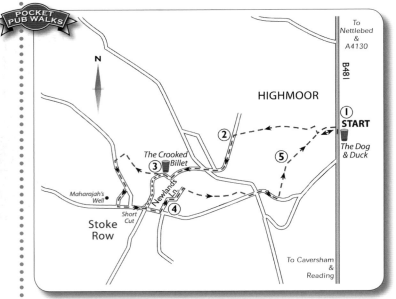

the hillside to cross three stiles in quick succession. Head diagonally left in the next field and exit via a stile to join a tarmac lane.

2 Turn left and pass a house on the left, followed by the entrance to **Little Farm**. Continue along the lane with the occasional house seen at the side of it. Cut through beech woodland and follow the bridleway down through the trees to a rough and rutted minor road. Cross over and immediately there is a path fork. Keep right, avoiding the bridleway, and follow the footpath through the trees. Soon a path crosses your route. Keep ahead with a white property seen over to the right across the paddock. Walk up to the main entrance to **Bushwood House** and swing left. Head for the next road and turn right. Beyond the **Crooked Billet pub** the road bends to the left.

The Maharajah's Well.

For the shorter route, walk into **Stoke Row** along the road. Go left at the junction for the **Cherry Tree pub** to reach Newlands Lane and continue from point 4.

To complete the full walk, as the road bends left swing right through a wrought iron kissing gate at the footpath sign and keep to the right-hand edge of a private garden.

3 Pass alongside several cottages and barns, go through a gate and keep ahead to the far right corner of an elongated pasture. Access into the next field is via a rather unusual roofed gateway, not unlike a churchyard lychgate. Look at the wall and you'll see a plaque which reads: 'Here lie the ashes of Michael Ian Fotherby 1953–2001. This gate was built by his wife and three sons in remembrance of happy times.' Veer left and head towards **Stoke Row Farm**. Cross the high stile and go forward up the slope towards the farm, passing through a galvanised gate and along a track with fields on the left. Keep the farmhouse on the right and at the next T-junction turn left. Pass an imposing gateway with brick and flint pillars and keep alongside a beech hedge. Immediately beyond the entrance to **Pond House** on the right, take the footpath also on the right and follow it along to the road at **Stoke Row**. Turn right and then right again to visit the **Maharajah's Well** and then return to the road, turn left and walk through the village. Pass **Coxs Lane** and the **Cherry Tree pub** to reach **Newlands Lane**.

4 Turn left here and follow the lane round to the right and then left. When it bends sharp left by a waymark, turn right, avoiding the path ahead going downhill. Cut through the trees, branching left at a footpath signpost. Descend through the woodland and soon a road is seen down below. Farther down is a cottage called **Bushwood**. Merge with the road, walk ahead and as it bends right, join a lane signposted to **Witheridge Hill**. Go uphill through the trees and as you break cover, just before a brick and flint house ahead on the bend, turn left onto a track. Branch half right after several paces at the sign for **Highmoor**. Follow the undulating path to a drive, keep left, then go right after several steps by the **Witheridge Hill Farm** sign. At the end of the drive, keep ahead on a path, cross a stile and continue ahead to cross a farm access road. Keep ahead in the next field, following the right-hand boundary.

5 Three-quarters of the way along you'll see a stile in the fence. Cross over and keep left to the next stile. Cross the next paddock, keeping to the right of a house and exit at the gate in the corner. Cross a drive and take the waymarked path, keeping alongside outbuildings and panel fencing. On reaching the intersection encountered in the early stages of the walk, turn right and retrace your steps to the road at **Highmoor**.

Places of interest nearby

Until mains water was piped to Stoke Row in 1906, the villagers used the **Maharajah's Well** to get their water. It comes as something of a surprise to visitors to find the well, enclosed by an exotic cupola, in the middle of the English countryside. In its day it yielded 600–700 gallons of water daily by way of a bucket pulley. It took ten minutes to wind the bucket each way. But what is the well's connection with India? Local resident Edward Anderdon Reade offered the Maharajah of Benares help and support when he was Lieutenant-Governor of the North-West Provinces in India and in return the Maharajah presented the village with a charitable gift – a much-needed well. Before that, local residents had relied on rainwater for their cooking and pond-water for washing. The well was officially opened on 24th May 1864 – Queen Victoria's birthday. There is unrestricted access to the Maharajah's Well.

The Dog

The delightful southern Chilterns are explored on this fine walk of varied delights. Beyond the village of Rotherfield Peppard, the route skirts a golf course to reach Greys Green. At this point there is the option to extend the ramble to visit one of the region's loveliest National Trust houses, Greys Court. Don't be surprised if you see 'health walks' logos and waymarks at intervals throughout the route. This health initiative was introduced by local GP Dr William Bird in 1996, and the benefits to his patients, who use specially produced leaflets to guide them round the countryside, are monitored at regular checkups. At the hamlet of Satwell, the walk passes the Lamb, one of the region's oldest pubs. These days the Lamb is run by the celebrity television chef Antony Worral Thompson.

Distance – 5 miles.

OS Explorer 171 Chiltern Hills West. GR 711818.

A walk through typical Chiltern country.

Starting point The Dog at Rotherfield Peppard.

How to get there *Take the B481 between Reading and Nettlebed and the Dog at Peppard is several miles to the south of the junction with the A4130, on the right if you are coming from Reading.*

THE PUB

Situated beside a spacious common, the **Dog** is a popular 'local' beloved of walkers, passing motorists and many more. The interior is quaint and cosy, with beams and an inglenook fireplace. Greene King IPA and Ruddles Best are the beers while the appetising menu includes such dishes as spaghetti bolognaise, lasagne, home-made lamb casserole, fish and chips, chilli con carne and sausage and mash with onion gravy. Sandwiches and a range of jacket potatoes and burgers are also on offer. Outside there are tables and benches at the front and a garden at the rear.

Open 11.30 am until 11 pm from Monday to Friday; 11 am until 11 pm on Saturday; 11.30 am until 10.30 pm on Sunday.
☎ *01491 628343*

[1] From the door of the **Dog** look for a footpath, a tarmac drive and a track. Take the latter on the extreme right. Pass some cottages, and a car park for the golf club is seen on the left along this stretch. Continue ahead over a golf course crossing and try your best to avoid serious muddy patches here and there. Pass a

bridleway on the right and take the next left bridle path. This is part of the **Chiltern Way**.

2. Keep the golf course on the left, pass over a tarmac drive and continue to the road. Turn right, pass a turning for **Shepherd's Green** and when you approach a sprawling expanse of grass on the left at **Greys Green**, you have a choice.

To visit **Greys Court**, follow the path to the right of the pavilion and down through woodland to a field. Keep ahead across the field, cross a lane and a few hundred yards beyond it is the house.

Otherwise turn immediately left onto a drive as you reach the green, pass **Greys Cottage** and walk ahead to a gate, joining an obvious path. Head for woodland and keep ahead, avoiding a path veering right. Beyond the trees, pass alongside paddocks and when you reach a smattering of houses and cottages at **Shepherd's Green**, cross the drive and look for a footpath sign pointing to the right.

3. Pass a property called **The Strip** on the right and follow the path to a gate and stile leading into a field. Avoid the path running

straight ahead down the pasture and keep left, passing a row of houses. Make for the stile in the field corner, aim slightly right in the next field to reach the corner of a wood and keep the trees on your left. Cross three more stiles before reaching woodland. Once in the trees walk ahead for about 75 yards, then turn left to pass between beeches and hollies. Head for the road, turn left, then immediately left along the lane to the **Lamb**.

The Lamb at Satwell.

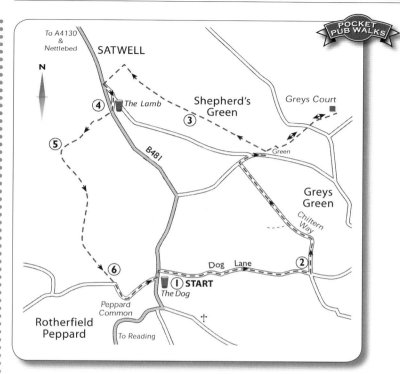

4 As you approach the pub, turn right at the junction and return to the B481. Cross over and take the bridleway opposite, passing to the right of a bungalow. Follow the path as it cuts through woodland and here and there are clumps of beech trees and holly bushes. Suddenly very tall beeches loom up in front of you, creating a cathedral-like canopy. White arrows painted on the tree trunks offer reassurance on this stretch. Head slightly south-west on the obvious path and when it forks, keep right. Go down to a crossroads where you will see the outline of a junction depicted on the bark of one of the trees. A tree-lined field can be glimpsed through the woodland here.

5 At this point turn left and walk through the wood. At length you emerge through the trees onto a clear path running between fields. Hedging and fencing line the route. Very soon you re-enter woodland, at this point almost rectangular in shape. Take either of the two paths cutting through the trees and you'll find you are heading in a general southerly direction. Eventually the routes meet up at the point where you reach a road on a bend.

6 Veer left here and follow the road uphill through the trees. Keep to the road as it sweeps left farther up, avoiding a lane running straight on by a 30 mile speed restriction sign. On the right now is the spacious green at the centre of **Rotherfield Peppard**. This is part of **Peppard Common**. Pass the **Red Lion** and recross the B481 to return to the **Dog**.

Places of interest nearby

Greys Court, now in the care of the National Trust, was originally a fortified manor. The present house is a gabled brick and flint construction dating back to the Elizabethan era. Greys Court and the village owe their name to Lord de Grey who fought at Crecy, became one of the original Knights of the Garter and was given a licence to crenellate the house in 1348. Greys Court includes a Tudor donkey-wheel well-house and the garden contains the Archbishop's Maze, whose design is based on the theme of reconciliation. In the early 18th century Greys Court passed to Sir William Stapleton whose descendants remained here until 1935. During the period the Stapletons occupied the estate, Greys Court consisted of 8,000 acres. Today, it is a more modest 300 acres.
☎ *01494 755564*

The Golden Ball

Many times over the years I have driven along the A4130 between Nettlebed and Henley though the landscape bisected by the road was unknown to me. Until now. This delightful walk, exploring the countryside where the Chilterns and Thames valley meet, gave me a completely new perspective on the area. To begin with, the distant hum of traffic on the A4130 is audible as you climb above Assendon, but the sound soon fades. The higher ground offers good views across to the corresponding slopes on the far side of the Fair Mile. The first of the Turkey oaks lining the path beside the road was planted by a young Princess Margaret in October 1953 to commemorate the Coronation of Queen Elizabeth II four months earlier. More than 50 years later, they have grown into mature trees.

Distance – 3¾ miles.

OS Explorer 171 Chiltern Hills West. GR 744847.

Various paths and tracks thread their way either side of the A4130 near Henley.

Starting point The Golden Ball at Lower Assendon.

How to get there *Follow the A4130 between Henley and Nettlebed and turn northwards onto the B480. If approaching from Henley, the B480 is along the Fair Mile on the right. The pub will be found on the left after a few hundred yards.*

If time permits you might like to make a day of it and visit Henley. On reaching the A4130 you can either walk into the town or catch the bus.

THE PUB There is a strong sense of history at the 400 year old **Golden Ball**. According to some sources, Dick Turpin hid in the priest hole here. Outside is a sunny south-facing garden, while indoors you'll find plenty of exposed timbers, a collection of old bottled ales and (in winter) an open fire. Current beers include Brakspear Bitter and Special, while the pub fare ranges from sausage and mash to fish pie.

Open 11 am to 3 pm and 6 pm to 11 pm throughout the week. Sunday hours are 12 noon to 3 pm and 7 pm to 10.30 pm.
☎ *01491 574157*

1 On leaving the pub turn right and follow the road for about 70 yards. Swing left at a lane and cross another minor road after a few paces to join a bridleway. Pass a house on the left called

Kings Ride, climb above the valley and follow the track to a hairpin bend. Keep ahead here, leaving the track to follow a broad sunken path through the trees. Extensive roots sprawl randomly in all directions. On the higher ground the path cuts between fields before reaching the entrance to **Henley Park** on the left. Turn right here, by a giant cedar tree, to pass through a kissing gate. You are now following a stretch of both the **Oxfordshire Way** and the **Seven Shires Way**. The latter route extends for 234 miles through Oxfordshire and six other counties – including Buckinghamshire, Warwickshire and Gloucestershire. Away to your left along here are glimpses of the **Thames valley**.

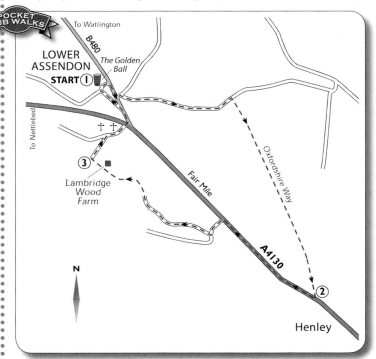

The Chilterns

The Fair Mile at Henley.

Go through a wrought iron kissing gate and as the track sweeps left by a barn, keep straight on along the grassy path. Stay on the path as it drops down into the valley, heading towards woodland. Descend a gentle slope to a wrought iron kissing gate and cut between the trees. Beyond them skirt a field with hedging on the left. Large Victorian villas on the outskirts of **Henley** make up the view ahead.

2 Turn right at the A4130, cross over by the speed camera and follow the tarmac path through the trees beside the **Fair Mile**. Pass a turning for several properties, including **Woodside**, **Willowdale** and **Barnfield**, and continue beyond the entrance to **Gable Cottage**. On reaching **Lambridge Wood Road**, turn left and pass a post box on the corner. After the road bends

left, look for a bridleway on the right, signposted to **Bix**. Follow the path between panel fencing and brick walls, leaving the outskirts of **Henley** behind you as you return to a rolling Chiltern landscape. Pass various houses on the left, which are soon replaced by woodland. Pass between beech trees, keeping right at a waymarked fork to skirt the wood. Pass lines of larch and silver birch trees and continue through mixed woodland to the buildings of **Lambridge Wood Farm** on the right.

3 Turn right just beyond them to follow a path that crosses the drive to the farm. Farther down the path descends into woodland before reaching the road. Cross with extreme care as it can be busy and take the B480 **Stonor** road. Veer left shortly by **Flint Cottage** to join a narrow lane and as it bends left, swing right through a gate into the garden of the **Golden Ball**.

Places of interest nearby

Henley – the name means 'at the high wood' – has much to offer the visitor. Probably its most famous landmark is the Thames yet there is much more to the town than our greatest river. Have a look at the 18th century bridge and you'll see there are carved masks on the keystones depicting Old Father Thames peering through bulrushes downstream and Isis looking upstream. The ford here was used during prehistoric times but the town itself is a medieval creation.

The **River and Rowing Museum** at Henley is well worth a visit. Open throughout the year, it illustrates Britain's impressive rowing heritage. Kenneth Grahame's much-loved characters from his classic children's story *The Wind in the Willows* are seen here as part of a spectacular walk-through attraction.
☎ *01491 415600*

15 Chazey Heath

The Pack Saddle

The first time I set foot in Mapledurham, midway round this walk, was during the very hot summer of 1976. I went to watch the village being used as a prominent film location in the famous adventure movie *The Eagle has Landed* based on a best-selling novel by Jack Higgins about a plot to kidnap Winston Churchill while he was spending the weekend at a country house in Norfolk in 1943. As someone with a keen interest in films and film-making, I think it would be fair to say that ever since that first visit, the village has had a strong, somewhat curious hold over me. Every time I go back, I am reminded of its major role in this film and in other movie and television productions.

Some of the scenes in *The Eagle has Landed* were shot by the 15th century corn mill, which includes two pairs of millstones used to produce wholemeal flour. Elsewhere in Mapledurham, there were significant changes. The village name changed to 'Studley Constable', an old fashioned dairy shop displayed gleaming milk-churns in the window and several baby Austins added to the nostalgic picture of rural England. There were even signposts indicating the east-coast port of King's Lynn! As you return to Chazey Heath you can see a picturesque cottage across the fields. In the film this is where two characters, a British spy and an American serviceman, meet a violent end.

THE PUB There has been a pub on this site since 1665. The road outside used to be a drovers' route between Reading and Oxford so the **Pack Saddle** was widely known as a convenient watering hole. It is still a popular haunt today, beloved of walkers, cyclists and passing motorists. Inside are two bars.

Distance – 6½ miles.

OS Explorer 159 Reading, Wokingham and Pangbourne. GR 695773.

Views of the Thames valley dominate this walk, which follows clear tracks and undulating field and golf course paths.

Starting point The Pack Saddle at Chazey Heath.

How to get there *Chazey Heath is on the A4074 between Caversham and Wallingford. Approaching from Reading, the turning for the Pack Saddle is signposted on the right just as you leave the built up area. There are three car parks offering a total of 100 spaces.*

The Chilterns

Wadworth 6X, IPA and JCB are the regular beers and among the popular dishes on the pub menu are cottage pie, bubble and squeak, ham, egg and chips and Sunday roast. Ploughman's lunches and baguettes are also available.

Open from 12 noon until 3 pm and 6 pm until 12 midnight on Monday to Thursday; 12 noon until 12 midnight on Friday, Saturday and Sunday.
☎ *01189 463000*

1 From the **Pack Saddle** cross the A4074 with care and take the road opposite signposted '**Mapledurham House**' and '**Water Mill**'. Over on the right, half hidden among the trees, is a small thatched cottage. About 100 yards along the road is a left-hand

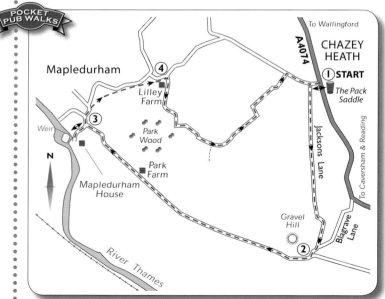

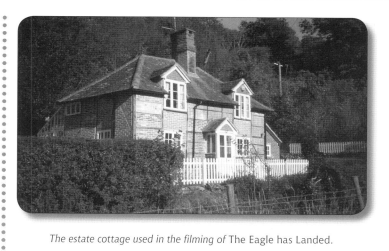

The estate cottage used in the filming of The Eagle has Landed.

bridleway. Take it and head south towards **Caversham** on the outskirts of Reading. Follow the track alongside the fairways and greens of a local golf club, head straight on at an intersection, by a cottage called **Three Chimneys**, and further on the right of way narrows to a path cutting between trees and fences. Pass a path on the right before reaching a lane on a bend by some houses. Keep right at this point, following **Blagrave Lane**, and when the road bends sharp left by **Gravel Hill Cottages**, go straight on at the footpath and bridleway signs.

2 Follow the path round to the right after a few paces and then descend quite steeply through a tunnel of trees. Turn right farther down at a junction with a track and follow it alongside woodland. The scenery on this stretch of the walk comprises fields and meadows strewn along the floor of the **Thames valley**. On reaching **New Lodge**, follow the track to the left of it, heading towards **Mapledurham House** in the distance. Walk along the track to **Park Farm** and then continue to the road just beyond a telephone box.

The Chilterns

3 Turn left to have a look at the mill, the house and the church. Retrace your steps back along the road and continue northwards, passing a sign for the **Chiltern Way extension**. Pass through a galvanised kissing gate in the right-hand bank, follow the path alongside fencing and woodland and then make your way up the field slope. The cottage used as one of the settings in *The Eagle has Landed* can now be seen on the left. Pass through a gate at the top of the field, walk ahead to the road and follow it ahead for about 100 yards to **Lilley Farm**.

4 Turn right to join a bridleway, keep left at the fork some way further on and walk down to some farm outbuildings. Head straight on at the **Chiltern Way** sign, turn left at a junction with a track and pass a 'private – no access' sign on the right. Take the next waymarked path on the right and follow it to the road. Turn right and return to the **Pack Saddle** on the A4074.

Places of interest nearby

Mapledurham House dates back to the late 16th century and was completed by Sir Richard Blount for his Catholic family. Constructed of red brick with stone dressings, Mapledurham is one of the largest and best-known houses in this part of the country. Among a variety of features are a fascinating priest hole and an 18th century private chapel, which can be seen from the adjoining churchyard of St Margaret's. Mapledurham means 'settlement by the stream and maples'. The house is open between Easter and September. River Thames boat trips between Caversham and Mapledurham House operate at weekends in the summer months.
☎ *01189 723350*